the Malecón, Havana, Cuba

A TRAVEL PHOTO ART BOOK

LAINE CUNNINGHAM

The Malecón, Havana, Cuba

A Travel Photo Art Book

Published by Sun Dogs Creations
Changing the World One Book at a Time
Print ISBN: 978-1-951389-22-2

Cover Image by Laine Cunningham
Cover Design by Angel Leya

Copyright © 2024 Laine Cunningham

All rights reserved. No part of this book may be reproduced in any form or by any means, electronic, mechanical, digital, photocopying or recording, except for the inclusion in a review, without permission in writing from the publisher.

Havana's Malecón offers a broad walkway atop the seawall that protects the island. Originally begun as a temporary construction, the Malecón shuttles car and foot traffic along five miles of the island's coast. A journey takes people from the mouth of the Havana Harbor down to the Almendares River, offering views of Old Havana, Centro Habana, and Vedado, each with its own flavor.

The Malecón took more than fifty years to build. Today, the area is so popular with locals it's called "the couch of Havana." Once the sun passes its peak, groups sit atop the seawall and enjoy the cool breezes. At certain times of the year, waves crash into the wall and send up spectacular sprays.

A number of monuments, including one to the victims of the USS *Maine*, stand near the water. Other points of interest include a statue honoring Cuban national hero José Martí. The most beautiful attractions are natural. The water changes color according to the weather, and the sunsets are not to be missed. After dark, the lights of the city enchant locals and visitors alike. Turn the page to begin your own private tour.

BRONZE

FLAGSHIP

TETRIS

FROTH

SPOTS

AIREDALE

WISP

IRL

LAERDAL

VIEWFINDER

SKETCH

WASHED

FLY

TOADSTOOL

FLORIDA

BATTLESHIP

TOKYO SUBWAY

ACTUATE

CAVALRY

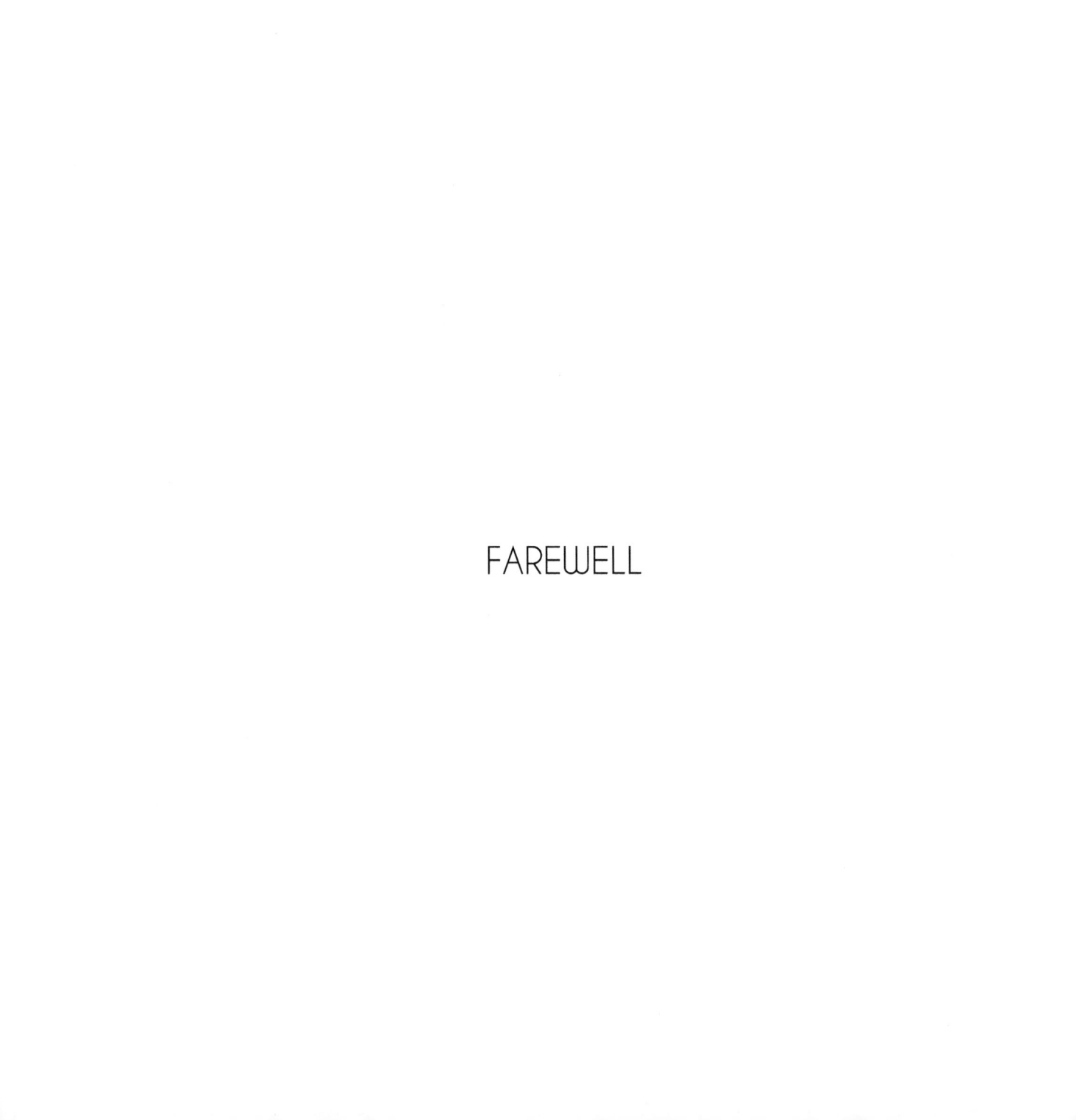

FOLK

LOCKBOX

INTERSECT

HUSH

WATCHFUL

SURREAL

WINDSAIL

PUCK

OUTTAKE

ARC

KINSHIP

GRIDWORK

STUDY

BRASS

FROSTED

JAWBONE

PERSPECTIVE

SKYWARD

OUTPOST

CORE

DALMATION

TOLKIEN

WEDDING CAKE

SUNDAY

NEBULA

TITLES IN THIS SERIES

Havana, Cuba
Old Havana, Cuba
The Malecón, Havana, Cuba
Central Havana, Cuba
Vedado, Havana, Cuba
Regla, Havana, Cuba
Miramar, Havana, Cuba
Streets of Havana, Cuba
Classic Cars of Cuba
Classic Cars of Old Havana, Cuba
Classic Cars of Havana, Cuba
Spanish Colonial Havana, Cuba
Gardens of Havana, Cuba
Verge Gardens of Havana, Cuba
Cats of Havana, Cuba
Colón Cemetery, Cuba
Havana Art School

www.ingramcontent.com/pod-product-compliance
Lightning Source LLC
Chambersburg PA
CBHW040002080526
44586CB00027B/2847